LOAN APPROVAL SIMPLIFIED

LOAN APPROVAL SIMPLIFIED

CA PRABHAT AGRAWAL

Worldwide Published by
Pendown Press

PENDOWN PRESS LLP
An ISO 9001 & ISO 14001 Certified Co.,
Regd. Office: 3767A, Kanhaiya Nagar,
Tri Nagar, Delhi-110035
Ph.: 8130886000, 9650072927
E-mail: info@pendownpress.com
Branch Office: 1A/2A, 20, Hari Sadan, Ansari Road,
Daryaganj, New Delhi-110002
Ph.: 011-45794768
Website: PendownPress.com

Edition: 2024
Price: ₹ 299
ISBN: 978-93-6338-434-7

Layout and Cover Designed by Pendown Graphics Team
Printed and Bound in India by Thomson Press India Ltd.

Dedications

I dedicate this book to my father, late Shri Badri Prasad. His teachings on hard work and never giving up have been very important to me.

To my mother, late Shakuntala Agrawal, whose lessons on fiscal prudence and sagacity have left a lasting imprint on me.

And to my beloved wife, Sonal Agrawal,whose enduring love and unwavering support have been my pillars.

Further, I extend my gratitude to Mr. Atul Banshal, Director of Finance Omaxe Ltd, India's premier Real Estate company. His profound knowledge of the Real Estate industry has significantly enriched the narrative of this book.

This book is a tribute to each of you and your contributions to shaping my character. Your affection, guidance, and backing have played a pivotal role in my accomplishments, and I am profoundly grateful for your presence in my life. May this book offer insights and assistance to its readers, serving as a testament to your profound influence on my journey.

Contents

Acknowledgements

I wish to take a moment to express my profound appreciation to those whose contributions have been pivotal in bringing this book to fruition.

Foremost, my heartfelt gratitude goes to Akshar Yadav, Pawan Wadhawan, and Naveen Banura, whose inspiration sparked the journey of writing this book and whose unwavering encouragement and support sustained me throughout.

My deepest thanks also go to my dear friend, Jai Sethi & Prashant Pandey, who have been constant sources of support and cherished presences in my life.

A special thanks to my friend, Dinesh Verma, CEO of Pendown Press, and his team for their constant support and suggestions throughout the creative process.

To each of these individuals, I owe an immense debt of gratitude for their steadfast support and meaningful contributions to the realization of this project.

And lastly, I would like to express my sincere appreciation to Kirandeep Chahal for her invaluable assistance in completing this book.

Thank you!

Prabhat Agrawal

About the Author

Prabhat Agrawal is the owner of **People Financials**, a company specializing in loans for the past 12 years. He is a chartered accountant by qualification and has been active in this field for the past 20 years. Previously, he spent 8 years at ICICI Bank, where he served as the Regional Manager for the loans division.

Prabhat's interest in the loan sector began during his tenure at ICICI Bank's loan division, where he worked in various departments such as credit, sales, and operations, gaining comprehensive knowledge of the retail loan industry. After becoming an expert in the field, he decided to pursue his passion for assisting people in obtaining loans through a simplified process by establishing his own venture by the name of **PEOPLE FINANCIALS.**

People Financials has partnered with 78 banks and financial institutions to provide loan facilities to customers, offering a wide range of retail loans, including Home Loans, LAP,

DOD Limit, OD/CC Limit, Unsecured Business Loans, Personal Loans, CGTSME Loans, Project Loans, Startup Funding, Car Loans, Education Loans, and Solar Power Loans. They aim to secure the best deals for customers through their extensive offerings in the market.

Prabhat's extensive experience in the industry, combined with his commitment to helping others achieve their financial goals, has established him as a trusted and knowledgeable resource. His expertise in understanding the importance of credit scores, particularly in today's world, where they play a crucial role in loan approvals, makes him invaluable to anyone seeking to improve their credit standing.

Preface

Welcome to **Loan Approval Simplified!**

In today's world, understanding your CIBIL score is more important than ever. Whether you're planning to buy a house, start a business, or simply manage your finances better, having a good CIBIL score can make a big difference. This book is here to help you navigate this crucial aspect of your financial journey.

We'll start by explaining what a CIBIL score is and why it matters. You'll learn how your score is calculated and how it impacts your ability to get loans. We've included practical tips and strategies to improve your score and maintain it, so you can make the most of your financial opportunities.

You'll also find real-life examples and case studies that show how others have successfully improved their CIBIL scores. These stories will inspire and guide you as you work on your own credit.

Our goal is to make understanding and improving your CIBIL score as simple as possible. We want you to feel confident and empowered to take control of your financial future.

Thank you for choosing this book as your guide. Let's get started on the path to financial success together!

Introduction

Hello, my name is Prabhat Agrawal.

I am a Chartered Accountant and former banker, specializing in the field of loans and borrowing. CIBIL plays a crucial role in this area, and my journey in the loan sector began early in my career as a banker, twenty years ago. Ever since then, it has never failed to impress me, both in building lasting relationships with my clients and in generating leads for my business.

I live and breathe borrowing strategy and CIBIL daily, and it continues to be one of my top tools for delivering measurable results. Throughout my experience, I have effectively utilized CIBIL tools to grow my business through strategic borrowing, helping countless small business owners, startups, and entrepreneurs optimize their borrowing approaches. The journey so far has been nothing short of remarkable!

But to truly understand my passion and commitment, let me share a bit more about where I come from.

I belong to a small city in Bihar, Muzaffarpur, where I completed my studies up to the 10th grade. My father, Late Shri Badri Prasad, was involved in the business of paper trading and manufacturing exercise books. I learned a lot from him. He was a deeply compassionate man who always believed in helping others and doing good. His values of kindness and integrity were his guiding principles, and he taught me to follow these values in everything I do.

Inspired by his lifestyle, I kept these values in mind when I came to Delhi to pursue further studies. I completed my studies in 2002, became a Chartered Accountant, and began my career at ICICI Bank, eager to make a difference in the financial world. While working there, I observed various aspects of the banking system and noticed some challenges.

Many customers were dealing with high interest rates and fees, as well as issues related to loan processing.

These challenges made me realize that there was an opportunity to make a positive change. I wanted to create a place where people could access fair and honest financial services without the complications I had observed. While working at the bank, I tried to address these issues to some extent, but system constraints limited my efforts.

So, I decided to leave my job and start my venture, People Financials, to resolve and help with issues related to finance. My mission with People Financials is to offer clear and transparent services that genuinely benefit our clients. We focus on providing customized loan solutions tailored to each client's needs, maintaining communication with them at every stage of the loan process, securing the best terms, and offering after-sales services throughout the loan's duration. Our goal is to make the loan process as straightforward and smooth as possible for everyone who comes to us.

By starting People Financials, I wanted to honour the lessons my father taught me. I strive to ensure that every client receives honest, helpful, and respectful service. It's about continuing the legacy of compassion and integrity that my father instilled in me and applying it to help people meaningfully. Whenever I help a client fulfill their requirements on terms suitable to them, it gives me a great sense of satisfaction. When they appreciate my work, it fills me with pride. I always work toward solving clients' problems and meeting their needs, rather than pushing them to take products that are not suitable for them.

For example, Mr. Ahuja, a client of ours, was struggling with limited funds and was unable to secure the necessary funding for his business expansion. Despite trying with his banker, he couldn't get the funding he needed. We came into contact with him through his CA, understood his business and challenges, and, with our expertise, secured funding for him within seven days, fully meeting his requirements.

Over the years, he has continued to receive funding and has increased his group's turnover from 10 crore to 40 crore within three years with the additional funding.

I trust that the insights shared in this book will guide you toward success in navigating borrowing strategies and understanding CIBIL.

Let's begin!

Here are 12 simple lessons I've learned about CIBIL that can help you with your borrowing plans.

Warm regards,

Mr. Prabhat Agrawal

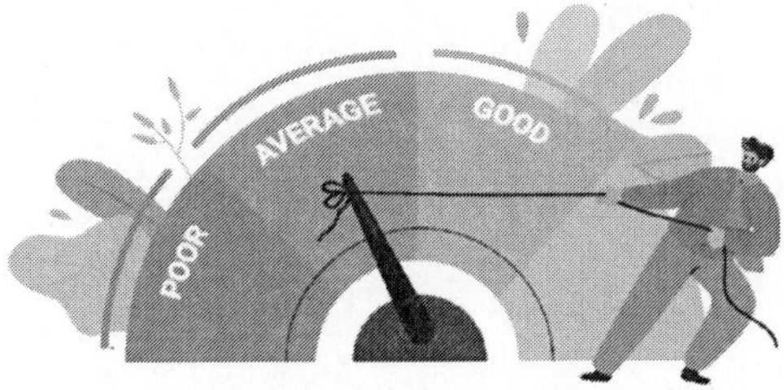

CHAPTER 1

What is the **CIBIL Score?**

CIBIL Score is a method that banks use to determine your loan payment history based on your current & past loan data gathered from different banks. In addition to evaluating your payment history, banks also determine your loan payment capacity or creditworthiness. Private companies like CIBIL, Experion, TransUnion, & other similar firms carry this out. These companies collect your data from various banks on specified dates and input it into your credit history through the software they use. Based on your data and repayment history, a score is then calculated.

Calculating Credit Score

Determining your credit score involves evaluating various factors to assess your creditworthiness, indicating to potential lenders the risk associated with extending credit or loaning money to you. This numerical representation is pivotal in financial transactions, as it reflects your reliability in meeting financial obligations.

Multiple elements are considered within the the formula used to compute your credit score, offering a comprehensive assessment of your financial profile.

For example, in school or college, we earn a perfect score of 100 out of 100 by answering all questions correctly, and a score of 90 out of 100 if we make some mistakes. Similarly,

CIBIL scoring works by evaluating your loan repayment history to calculate your score.

If you repay all your loans on time, you will achieve the highest score. However, if you delay or miss payments, your score will decrease.

The CIBIL Score ranges between 300 to 900. The maximum CIBIL score one can achieve is 900, while a score of 750 and above is considered good by banks. Anything less than 750, may prompt banks to request justification. CIBIL scores of 800 and above are considered very good by banks, akin to scoring in the 90th percentile in an exam.

Mr. Ajay, an esteemed client working at Oracle, has taken two home loans and one car loan, consistently repaying all EMIs on time. While he rarely experiences any delays throughout the tenure, he consistently pays all EMIs and credit card bills on time, resulting in a CIBIL score of 805.

Only 10% - 15% of CIBIL scores are in the range of more than 800, 40% - 50% are in the range of 750-800, 10% - 15% are between 700-750, and the remaining scores are less than 700.

Factors Affecting Your Credit Score

1. **Credit Card Utilization:** This refers to the percentage of your available credit that you are using. Keeping your utilization low (typically below 30%) can positively impact your score.
2. **Payment History:** Timely payments are crucial for a healthy credit score. Late or missed payments can significantly lower your score and reflect poorly on your creditworthiness.

3. **Age of Credit Lines:** The longer your credit history, the better it is for your credit score. Older accounts show your ability to manage credit over time.
4. **Credit Inquiries:** Each time you apply for credit, a hard inquiry is recorded. Multiple inquiries in a short period can negatively affect your score, as it may signal financial stress.
5. **Total Accounts:** Having a variety of credit accounts, such as loans, mortgages, and credit cards, can boost your score by showing your ability to handle different types of credit responsibly.
6. **Negative Status Accounts:** Accounts with negative marks, like defaults, bankruptcies, or accounts sent to collections, can drastically lower your credit score. Managing these effectively or resolving them quickly is essential for improving your credit health.

CHAPTER 2

Understanding Your CIBIL Report

Your CIBIL report is a detailed record of your credit history prepared by a credit bureau. In India, the most recognized credit bureau is CIBIL (Credit Information Bureau (India) Limited). This report includes information about your credit accounts, payment history, and any outstanding debts.

Understanding your credit report is crucial for managing your financial health and improving your CIBIL score. By reviewing your report regularly, you can identify any discrepancies, track your credit utilization, and ensure that your financial practices align with your goals.

How to Access Your CIBIL Report

Regularly accessing and reviewing your CIBIL report helps you stay informed about your credit status and ensures that all information is accurate and up-to-date.

Here's how you can access your CIBIL report and what to do once you have it:

- **Requesting Your Report:** You can obtain your CIBIL report online through the official CIBIL website. You'll need to provide some personal details and verification documents. You're entitled to one free credit report once a year, but you can also opt to purchase additional reports if needed.
- **Reviewing the Report:** Once you receive your report, carefully review each section. Pay special attention to any discrepancies or unfamiliar accounts.
- **Disputing Errors:** If you find errors in your report, you can raise a dispute with CIBIL. This process involves submitting proof of the error and following up to ensure that corrections are made.

Understanding Your CIBIL Score:

Your CIBIL score, which ranges from 300 to 900, is a numerical representation of your creditworthiness. A higher score indicates a better credit health. Here's what you need to know:

Score Ranges

- **300-549: Poor –** You may face difficulties in obtaining credit.
- **550-649: Fair –** You might get credit, but on less favorable terms.
- **650-749: Good –** You are likely to receive credit at competitive rates.
- **750-900: Excellent –** You have a strong credit profile and will qualify for the best terms.

Key Components of a CIBIL Report:

Understanding your CIBIL report is essential for managing your credit health effectively. The report is a detailed snapshot of your credit history and provides insights into various aspects of your financial behavior. By familiarizing yourself with the key components of your CIBIL report, you can better assess your creditworthiness, identify areas for improvement, and ensure that all the information is accurate.

Here are the key components of a CIBIL report:

- **Personal Information:** This section contains your name, date of birth, address, and contact details. Ensure that all this information is correct to avoid any confusion.
- **Credit Accounts:** This includes details about your credit cards, loans (personal, home, auto), and any other lines of credit. It shows your credit limit, the current balance, and the payment history for each account.

- **Credit Inquiries:** This section lists all the inquiries made by lenders when you apply for credit. Too many inquiries in a short period can negatively impact your score.
- **Public Records:** This includes information about bankruptcies, foreclosures, or any other public records related to your financial behavior.
- **Collections:** If you have any accounts that have been sent to collections due to non-payment, they will be listed here.

Importance of Regularly Checking Your Credit Report

- **Identify Errors:** Mistakes in your credit report can lower your score. Regularly reviewing your report helps you spot and correct errors promptly.
- **Prevent Fraud:** Monitoring your report can help you detect any fraudulent activities, such as accounts opened in your name without your knowledge.
- **Improve Financial Planning:** Understanding your credit report helps you plan better for future credit needs and improve your financial habits.

Regularly checking your credit report is essential for maintaining accurate credit records and protecting against fraud. By spotting and correcting errors early, you can prevent unnecessary impacts on your credit score and make more informed financial decisions. Make it a habit to review your report regularly to ensure your financial health remains in top shape.

CHAPTER 3

How Can We Get a Good CIBIL Score?

Achieving a good CIBIL score is crucial for accessing favorable credit terms and securing financial stability. A higher score opens doors to better loan conditions and lower interest rates. This chapter outlines essential strategies to help you improve and maintain a healthy CIBIL score.

There are several ways to get a good CIBIL score.

- **Timely Payments:** The foundation of your credit score rests significantly on your payment track record. Be it settling utility bills, credit card statements, loan installments, or any other financial obligation, ensure prompt payments without delay. Simplify this process by setting up automatic payments or utilizing reminders to stay on top of due dates.

- **Start with Small Loans/Credit cards:** Additionally, abstaining from taking loans or using credit cards is not a method for maintaining a good CIBIL score, as a lack of credit history results in a score of zero or negative. Banks do not view a zero or negative CIBIL score favorably, as they cannot assess creditworthiness. In such cases, the best approach is to obtain a credit card, make some purchases, and ensure timely repayment to avoid a zero-credit score.

- **Credit Utilization Ratio:** This ratio compares the amount of credit you're currently using to the total amount of credit available to you. Keeping this ratio low can positively impact your credit score.

- **Avoid applying with Many banks:** To improve your credit score, you should avoid applying for loans with many banks at the same point in time. Each application results in a credit inquiry, which can reduce your score by some points.

- **Review your CIBIL Report:** To improve your CIBIL score, obtain our credit report from one of the major credit bureaus & look for areas that need improvement, such as high credit utilization or late payments. Also, review your credit report to identify any errors or inaccuracies that might be negatively impacting your credit score. Raise a dispute for any errors or inaccuracies with the credit bureaus & follow up with them until the corrections are made. You can also seek professional help for the same if you face any problems.

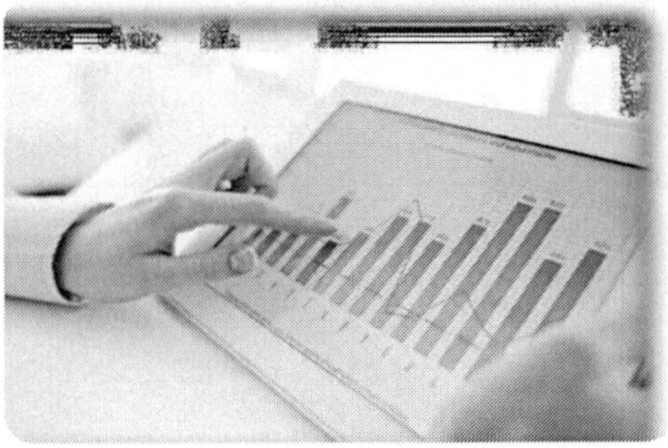

- **Paying Off Bad Loans and Credit Cards:** Paying off some of the bad loans and credit cards that are majorly affecting your CIBIL score would be a good idea to improve your credit score.

Improving your credit score is a gradual process that requires patience and consistency. Set realistic goals and remain committed to these practices for long-term success.

Additionally, based on my experience, I can assert that to ensure timely payment of all loans, certain considerations must be kept in mind, which I will elaborate on in the next chapter.

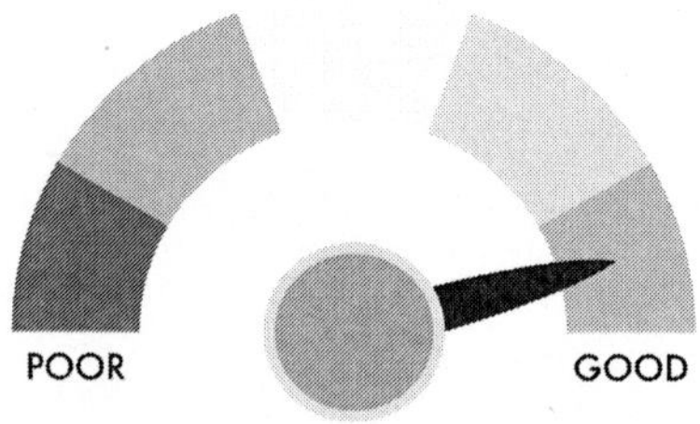

CHAPTER 4

Things to Keep in Mind for Paying All Loans on Time

While repaying your current loans, although you intend to pay them all on time and maintain a good CIBIL Score, sometimes it may not turn out as planned.

There are several reasons why you might not be able to maintain a good repayment record required for a CIBIL score:

1. **Your ECS Was Not Executed Properly:** When repaying your loan EMIs, banks execute ECS (Electronic Clearance Services) from your existing banker to receive their EMIs regularly on the due date. However, due to reasons like signature mismatch, an OD (overdraft) account, or other issues with the account, ECS execution may fail, and the bank is unable to receive the EMI on time. In such cases, it's necessary to ensure proper ECS execution to ensure timely payments from the next month. If you have only an OD account in the name of the company then you should open a current account with the bank & start ECS payments through this account, as ECS cannot be executed through an OD account.
2. **You Forgot to Maintain a Sufficient Balance in Your Account from Which the EMI Is Being Debited:** Sometimes, we forget to maintain a sufficient balance in the account from which the EMI is debited, especially if we don't frequently use that account. To prevent this, it's important to establish mechanisms to fund the account on time so that you do not miss paying EMI on time. Keeping one EMI in advance

in that account is a very good idea to overcome this issue. Also, setting a reminder one day before the EMI date to fund that account can be done to overcome this issue.

3. **Repayment from the Business Account to Vendors Using Issued Cheques:** In business transactions, we often issue cheques to vendors without considering when those cheques will be deposited. Sometimes, even though we have enough balance in our account for the EMI, a vendor's cheque may be deposited on the same date as the EMI date, causing the balance to fall below the required EMI level. To avoid this situation, it's crucial to calculate and maintain balances considering both vendor cheques and EMI amounts.

4. **Accuracy:** Ensure that all information on your credit report is accurate. Errors Could negatively impact your credit score.

There are numerous additional reasons, but space limitations prevent me from listing them all here.

CHAPTER 5

Optimizing Credit Utilization

This chapter explores the crucial topic of credit utilization and how it affects your credit scores and ability to borrow money. The ratio of your outstanding credit amounts to your available credit limits is known as credit utilization. When determining your creditworthiness, credit scoring models take this important feature into account.

Effectively managing your credit utilization ratio is crucial for elevating your credit score and enhancing your ability to borrow.

Here, we look at methods for maximizing the advantages of this ratio and managing it well:

- **Comprehending Credit Utilization Ratio:** This figure is arrived at by dividing the total amount of debt owed on all of your credit accounts by the total amount of credit limits that are accessible to you. For instance, your credit utilization ratio would be 20%, if your total credit limit is Rs. 1,00,000 and you owe Rs. 20,000 on your accounts.
- **The influence on credit scores is significant:** Upholding a low credit utilization ratio is crucial for attaining and sustaining a commendable credit score. Elevated utilization ratios may signal financial stress or imprudent financial management to creditors, potentially resulting in a diminished credit score. As a general guideline, it is advisable to maintain your credit utilization below 40%-50%, with lower ratios typically yielding more favorable outcomes.

Managing Credit Utilization Strategies

- **Reducing Balances:** An efficient method to decrease your credit utilization ratio involves paying off existing balances on your credit accounts promptly.

- **Enhancing Credit Limits:** Another viable tactic is to seek increases in credit limits on your current accounts. This can effectively lower your utilization ratio, provided that you don't correspondingly escalate your spending.
- **Opening New Credit Lines:** While opening fresh accounts can expand your overall available credit, it's imperative to approach this cautiously. It's worth noting that doing so may temporarily lower your credit score due to credit inquiries and a reduction in average account age.
- **Regular Monitoring and Adjustment:** Consistently monitoring your credit utilization ratio and making necessary adjustments are essential. Strive to maintain low balances relative to your credit limits across all your accounts.

Impact on Borrowing Capacity

Sustaining a healthy credit utilization ratio not only enhances your credit score but also bolsters your borrowing capacity.

Lower utilization ratios are generally viewed favorably by

lenders as they signify responsible credit management and reduced risk.

By understanding the importance of credit utilization and implementing effective management strategies, you can optimize your credit scores, enhance your financial standing, and unlock better borrowing opportunities. In the following sections of this book, we will delve deeper into each strategy, offering practical tips and insights for managing credit utilization effectively.

CHAPTER 6

How to Maintain a Good CIBIL Score

To maintain a good CIBIL score, one crucial factor, apart from paying on time, is to having a diverse mix of loans. Lenders prefer to see how you handle different types of loans responsibly, which is why having a variety of loans can positively impact your credit score. In this chapter, we will explain the different types of loans that you can mix to improve your CIBIL better.

Different Types of Loan Mix

Mortgage Loans:

1. These loans are provided against the security of a property, which is mortgaged while taking the loan. Examples include home loans, commercial property purchases, or industrial property purchases.

   Another way of taking these loans is to mortgage existing property you have & take the loan. Mortgage loans typically have longer repayment periods, which impacts your CIBIL for a longer duration.

2. **Unsecured Loans:**

   These loans do not require any security to be mortgaged and are given based on your business strength. Examples include business loans, personal loans, and CGTSME loans.

Unsecured loans generally have shorter repayment periods, and their EMIs are usually higher due to the short term. These loans are significant in assessing your behavior with unsecured credit and how you manage higher EMIs.

Credit Cards

There is a common misconception that using a credit card does not constitute a loan. However, credit card usage plays a significant role in determining your CIBIL score. Credit cards involve revolving credit, where you make purchases and pay on due dates as specified.

All three types of loans have different payment cycles and affect behavior that highly impacts your CIBIL score. To maintain a good CIBIL Score, it is beneficial to have a mix of all these loan types, so bankers can see your repayment behavior across various types of loans.

Also, having a mix of different loan types helps because your behavior with each type of loan is already reflected in your CIBIL report when you apply for that loan again.

For Example: Bankers while assessing unsecured loan applications may hesitate to approve them if you have only had secured loans in the past. Since unsecured loans are considered high-risk, lenders will be unable to assess your repayment behavior for this type of loan based on past performance alone, and therefore might be reluctant to approve the application.

CHAPTER 7

Influential Variables Impacting Your CIBIL Report

Avoid Excessive Loan Inquiries: Another crucial factor in maintaining a good CIBIL Score is to avoid excessive loan inquiries & loan applications. While applying for a loan, many people mistakenly apply with multiple banks to get the best deal. However, this can negatively impact your CIBIL score. Each time you apply for a loan, your CIBIL score is checked by banks, and multiple inquiries can lower your score. A high number of inquiries in your CIBIL history can be viewed negatively by lenders.

Settlement of Loans: Another important factor to keep in mind for maintaining your CIBIL is to avoid settlement of any loans / Credit card payments for whatever reason it may be. It can significantly impact your CIBIL report & you may lead to denial I of loans or credit cards in the future.

While settling disputed loans or credit card payments might seem like an easy solution, it is recorded in your CIBIL history and is viewed unfavorably by banks. To prevent this, pay off any small outstanding amounts in full to avoid having the term "settlement" appear in your CIBIL report.

Take advantage of Credit Monitoring Services: Many well-established companies offer credit monitoring services that provide timely alerts regarding any alterations or questionable activities on your credit report. These services frequently incorporate identity theft safeguards and credit score monitoring, presenting thorough monitoring options.

Manage Credit Scores: It's important to stay vigilant about your credit score, as it can serve as an early warning system for potential issues. Abrupt declines in credit scores may indicate fraudulent activities or errors on your credit report, prompting you to investigate further.

Review Account Statements Carefully

Alongside monitoring credit reports, it is essential to regularly scrutinize your bank and credit card statements. Look out for any unfamiliar transactions or discrepancies that could point to fraudulent behavior.

Activate Fraud Alerts: Many credit bureaus offer the option to activate fraud alerts on your credit report. These alerts notify you of any suspicious activity, such as new account openings or significant changes to existing accounts, enabling you to respond promptly to potential threats.

Consider Professional Assistance if Needed

If you find yourself overwhelmed by debt or struggling to improve your credit independently, it may be beneficial to seek help from reputable credit counseling agencies or financial advisors. They can offer personalized guidance and assist you in developing a realistic plan for debt repayment and credit enhancement.

By managing your credit utilization, avoiding excessive inquiries, and staying proactive with credit monitoring, you can significantly enhance and maintain a strong CIBIL score. Implementing these strategies will pave the way for better financial opportunities and a more stable credit profile.

CHAPTER 8

Common Myths About CIBIL Scores

Many misconceptions surround CIBIL scores, leading to confusion and poor financial decisions.

For example, some people think a CIBIL score is the only thing that matters for getting a loan, but lenders also look at your income, job stability, and credit history. Others believe that checking their own CIBIL score will hurt their credit, but this is not true—checking your score is a soft inquiry and does not affect it. Understanding these points can help you make better financial choices and improve your credit health. Let's debunk some of the common myths:

Myth 1: Checking Your Own CIBIL Score Lowers It

Fact: When you check your credit score, it is considered a "soft inquiry" and does not impact your score. Only "hard inquiries" made by lenders when you apply for credit can affect your score.

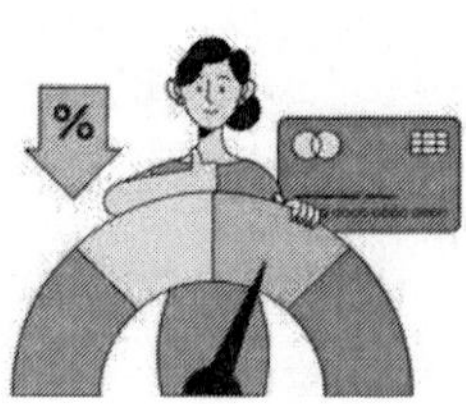

Myth 2: Closing Credit Cards Improves Your Score

Fact: Closing a credit card can lower your score by reducing your total available credit, thereby increasing your credit utilization ratio. It's better to keep old accounts open and maintain a low balance.

Myth 3: Only Late Payments Affect Your Score

Fact: While timely payments are crucial, other factors like credit utilization, length of credit history, types of credit, and recent credit inquiries also impact your score.

Myth 4: Paying Off Debt Automatically Erases It from Your Report

Fact: Paying off debt improves your financial health, but the history of that debt will remain on your credit report for seven years. This history can be positive if you've been making regular payments.

Myth 5: A Higher Income Guarantees a Higher Score

Fact: Your income does not directly affect your CIBIL score. The score is based on how well you manage your credit, not how much you earn.

By understanding the facts behind these myths, you can make more informed decisions to manage and improve your CIBIL score effectively.

Fixing Errors in Your CIBIL Report

Errors in your credit report can lower your CIBIL score and affect your ability to get credit. Here's how to identify and fix these errors:

Common Errors in Credit Reports

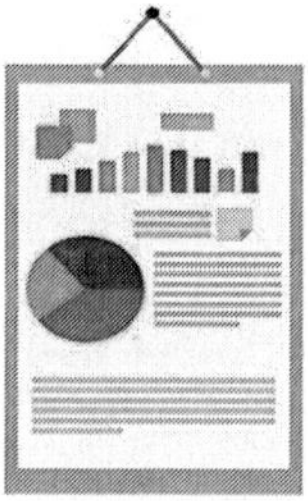

- **Incorrect Personal Information:** Mistakes in your name, address, or date of birth.
- **Errors in Account Information:** Incorrect account details, such as wrong account numbers or balances.

- **Duplicate Accounts:** The same account listed multiple times.
- **Incorrect Payment History:** Payments marked as late or missed when they were actually on time.
- **Unrecognized Accounts:** Accounts that do not belong to you, possibly due to identity theft.

Steps to Fix Errors

- **Review Your Credit Report:** Obtain a copy of your credit report from CIBIL and review it carefully for any errors.
- **Identify Errors:** Make a list of any inaccuracies you find in your report.
- **Gather Supporting Documents:** Collect documents that support your claim, such as payment receipts or bank statements.
- **Dispute the Errors:** Submit a dispute with CIBIL through their online portal or by mail. Include a detailed explanation of the error and attach supporting documents.
- **Follow Up:** Monitor the status of your dispute. CIBIL will investigate and make corrections if necessary. They will notify you once the investigation is complete.
- **Check the Updated Report:** After the errors have been corrected, obtain a new copy of your credit report to ensure the changes have been made.

By regularly checking your credit report and promptly fixing any errors, you can maintain a high CIBIL score and ensure your financial health is accurately represented.

CHAPTER 9

Benefits of Having a Good CIBIL Score

There are several benefits to maintaining a good CIBIL score. In this chapter of the book, I will discuss the same. One of the most important advantages is that it makes the loan-taking process smooth. If you have a good CIBIL history, banks view it positively when assessing your loan application, leading to quicker and easier approvals.

Additionally, there are other benefits of a good CIBIL score. Nowadays, most banks' interest rates for loans depend on the CIBIL score you have. If the CIBIL score is high, banks offer a lower rate of interest compared to a lower CIBIL score, where a higher rate of interest is charged.

For example, consider the case of a home loan: if your CIBIL score is more than 800, you will get the best interest rate available in the market. If your score is between 750-800, a premium of 0.05%-0.10% will be charged. If the CIBIL score is less than 750, then a premium of 0.10%-0.20% will be charged.

In the case of Major Banks, home loans with a CIBIL score above 800 have a rate of interest (ROI) of 8.60%, while those with a score between 750 and 800 are charged 8.70%, and those below 750 incur an 8.80% ROI.

There are several other benefits as well for having a good CIBIL score, which can be discussed.

Long-Term Benefits of a High CIBIL Score

Maintaining a high CIBIL score offers numerous long-term benefits, making it easier and cheaper to manage your finances. Here are some advantages:

1. **Lower Interest Rates:** Lenders offer lower interest rates to individuals with high CIBIL scores. This means you pay less interest over the life of a loan, saving you money.
2. **Easier Loan Approvals:** A high CIBIL score increases your chances of getting loan approvals. Lenders see you as a low-risk borrower, making them more willing to extend credit to you.
3. **Higher Credit Limits:** With a high CIBIL score, you are more likely to be offered higher credit limits on credit cards and loans. This gives you more financial flexibility.
4. **Better Credit Card Offers:** Credit card companies offer better terms, lower interest rates, and attractive rewards to individuals with high CIBIL scores. You may also qualify for premium credit cards with exclusive benefits.
5. **Favorable Terms on Mortgages:** A high CIBIL score can help you secure a mortgage with better terms, such as lower down payments and reduced closing costs.
6. **Employment Opportunities:** Some employers check credit scores during the hiring process, especially for jobs that require financial responsibility. A high CIBIL score can improve your job prospects.
7. **Peace of Mind:** Maintaining a high CIBIL score provides financial security and peace of mind. You'll be better prepared for emergencies and ensuring access to credit when you need it.

8. **Financial Flexibility:** A high CIBIL score gives you more options and flexibility in managing your finances. You can take advantage of better credit offers and make financial decisions with confidence.
9. **Visa Approvals:** Shortly, some visa approvals will be based on your credit score. It can be either approved or denied depending on your CIBIL score, so it's extremely important to keep your score in good shape.

By maintaining a high CIBIL score, you can enjoy these long-term benefits and achieve greater financial stability.

CHAPTER 10

How a Bad CIBIL Score Affects Your Borrowing Capacity

There are several benefits that we gain by maintaining a good CIBIL score. Conversely, there are significant negative impacts associated with having a bad CIBIL score. In this chapter of the book, I will discuss both aspects. One of the main problems of having a bad CIBIL score is that it affects our borrowing capability.

If we do not have a good CIBIL history, banks, while assessing our loan, view it negatively and hesitate to sanction the loan. In most cases, the loan is rejected.

Additionally, there are other negative consequences of a bad CIBIL score.

As explained earlier, nowadays most banks' Rate of Interest (ROI) for loans are dependent on the CIBIL score you have. If the CIBIL score is low, banks offer a higher ROI compared to a high CIBIL score where a lower ROI is charged.

Apart from these, in some cases, due to a poor credit history or financial situation, if the CIBIL score is not good, we might have to approach NBFCs (Non-Banking Financial Companies) for a loan, as banks may refuse to offer us one. Furthermore, NBFCs often charge very high interest rates and processing fees compared to banks as a penalty for a bad CIBIL score.

Examples of NBFCs include Tata Capital, Hero Housing, Cholamandalam Finance, L&T Finance, and several other similar financial institutions. There are several other problems we might face in running our business due to a bad CIBIL score, which, again due to space constraints, cannot be covered here.

CHAPTER 11

Real-Life Success Stories of Improving CIBIL Score

Hearing about real-life success stories can be motivating and provide valuable insights. Here are a few examples of individuals who improved their CIBIL scores through smart financial practices:

Story 1: From Poor to Excellent

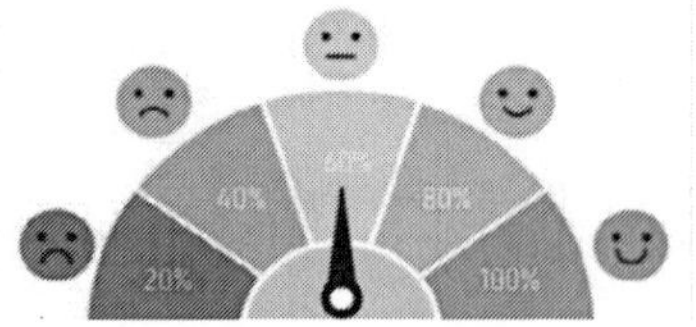

Anita had a poor CIBIL score due to missed credit card payments and a defaulted personal loan. Determined to improve her score, she started by paying off small debts first. She set up automatic payments for her bills and kept her credit card balances low. Within two years, her score improved from 550 to 750, allowing her to qualify for a home loan with a favorable interest rate.

Story 2: Overcoming a Financial Setback

Raj faced a financial setback when he lost his job and struggled to pay his bills. His CIBIL score dropped to 600. He worked with a credit counselor to create a debt management plan, negotiated with creditors for better terms, and took up a part-time job to increase his income. Over time, he paid off his debts, and his score improved to 720, enabling him to secure a personal loan to start his own business.

Story 3: Building Credit from Scratch

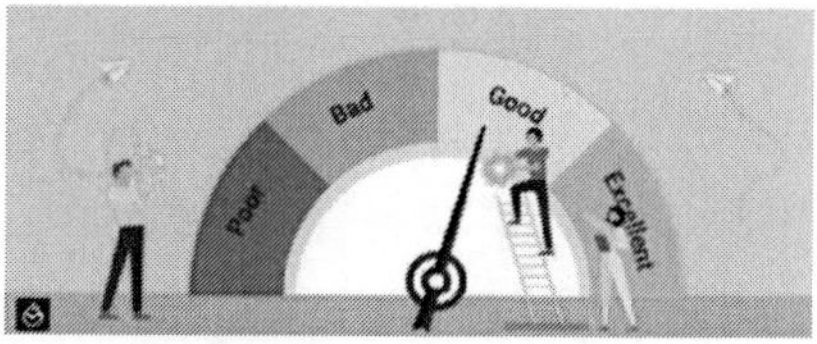

Priya, a young professional, had no credit history and a low CIBIL score of 650. She applied for a secured credit card and used it responsibly, paying the balance in full each month. She also took out a small personal loan and made timely payments. Within a year, her score increased to 700, making it easier for her to get an auto loan at a competitive rate.

Story 4: Recovering from Bankruptcy

After declaring bankruptcy, Manish's CIBIL score plummeted to 500. He was determined to rebuild his credit. He started by obtaining a secured credit card and making regular, on-time payments. He also took out a small, manageable loan and paid it off promptly. Through disciplined financial behavior, he raised his score to 680 in three years and was able to get a mortgage for a new home.

These stories show that with determination, discipline, and smart financial practices, it is possible to significantly improve your CIBIL score and achieve your financial goals.

CHAPTER 12

How Can the CIBIL Score Be Improved?

There are several ways to improve our CIBIL score, some of which have been explained in an earlier chapter. However, there are situations where our scores are low, and we can look to improve them.

Here, I will discuss these methods and also provide a case study of one of our clients, illustrating how we improved his CIBIL score & helped him secure a loan.

Guiding Principles for Restoring Credit Health

In this chapter, we will explore the fundamental strategies individuals can employ to restore damaged credit. The restoration of credit is paramount for securing financial stability and accessing favorable borrowing terms. By adhering to these guidelines, individuals can actively enhance their creditworthiness and overall financial well- being.

Establish Positive Payment Habits

Cultivating positive payment habits stands as a cornerstone in the journey of repairing damaged credit. This entails consistently making punctual payments across all active accounts, including credit cards, loans, and utility bills.

A steadfast commitment to timely payments showcases fiscal prudence and contributes to the gradual elevation of credit scores. If there are outstanding loans, initiating repayment is essential to rectify the situation.

Addressing Outstanding Debts

Effectively managing outstanding debts is a pivotal step in the credit repair process. Prioritize settling overdue debts or those in collections. Engaging with financial institutions to fully settle past debts is advised, and obtaining written confirmation of such settlements is crucial. By alleviating these financial obligations, individuals can markedly enhance their credit scores and underscore their dedication to financial accountability.

Dispute Loan Not Related to You

Sometimes due to errors by Credit Score Companies loans that do not pertain to you may appear in your CIBIL report. Check out your CIBIL properly & dispute any loans that are not yours and are negatively impacting your score. Ensure that these erroneous loans are removed from your CIBIL report.

Seek Professional Assistance if Necessary

Consider seeking professional assistance if necessary. Repairing damaged credit can sometimes be complex and demanding. In such instances, turning to credit counseling agencies or credit repair firms can prove advantageous. These experts offer tailored guidance, advocate with creditors on your behalf, and aid in devising a strategy for enhancing your credit standing. However, it's crucial to conduct thorough research and select reputable organizations to avoid scams or exacerbating financial woes.

By diligently adhering to these steps, individuals can steadily repair their impaired credit and pave the path toward a more robust financial future. It's important to bear in mind that patience and persistence are paramount, as credit restoration often unfolds gradually, necessitating unwavering dedication and discipline.

Case Study

Mr. Akash from Steel Mint applied for a loan with the bank, and the bank informed us that his CIBIL score is 652, which is quite low, so they cannot extend the loan to him. This came as a shock to him, as he was unaware of his low CIBIL score and its potential impact on his loan-taking capacity. He had already given an advance of Rs. 20 lakhs for the purchase of a house, and if his loan was not approved, he would not be able to purchase the house, and his Rs. 20 lakhs advance would be forfeited.

He did not have the details of the credit cards and could not pay the balances. Furthermore, the banks that had issued his credit cards had closed their operations in India and were sold to other banks, so he could not approach the respective banks either. He was unaware now how to proceed further to get these issues resolved and removed from CIBIL report. He sought our services for assistance.

We analyzed his CIBIL report in detail and found that the issues dated back to 2008 when Mr. Akash had lost his purse carrying several credit cards. Minimal outstanding balances had accumulated over the years, negatively impacting his CIBIL score.

We conducted a thorough analysis and identified the banks that still existed and accepted payments. We approached these banks, paid off the outstanding balances in full without any settlements, and successfully improved his credit score within 2 months.

Summary

- **Mastering the Art of CIBIL:** Understanding, Calculating, and Enhancing Your Score
- **From Good to Great:** Strategies for Elevating Your CIBIL Score and Securing Favorable Loan Terms
- **Empowering Financial Wellness:** Practical Insights and Real-Life Cases for CIBIL Score Enhancement

We have discussed what CIBIL is all about and how it is calculated. Additionally, we talked about how CIBIL impacts our borrowing capacity and ways to achieve a good CIBIL score. We also highlighted the important factors to keep in mind to ensure timely payment of loans, illustrated with the example of Mr. Vimal Kishore, who maintained his CIBIL score by paying his EMIs on time.

Furthermore, we discussed the benefits of having a good CIBIL score, such as banks being more comfortable in providing loans and offering lower rates of interest based on a good CIBIL score.

Conversely, we highlighted how a bad CIBIL score can negatively impact the rate of interest and loan borrowing capacity. Additionally, we discussed ways to improve our CIBIL score. Our discussion encompassed an in-depth analysis of CIBIL, unraveling its intricacies and calculation methodologies. We underscored its profound influence on borrowing capacity and financial well-being, emphasizing the importance of cultivating a robust CIBIL score.

Expert Guidance

Unlocking Financial Success with Professional Guidance

Your Path to Loan Approval! As you embark on your journey towards financial empowerment, it's essential to equip yourself with the right tools and resources to navigate the complex landscape of borrowing money. In today's world, where every financial decision matters, being well-informed and making strategic choices can make all the difference.

In **"Loan Approval Simplified,"** we've explored deep into the world of credit and lending, providing you with comprehensive insights into what CIBIL is and how it impacts your ability to secure loans. We've clarified the calculation methods behind CIBIL scores and highlighted the crucial role they play in determining your borrowing capacity.

Throughout the book, we've emphasized the importance of maintaining a good CIBIL score and outlined practical strategies for achieving and maintaining it. From understanding the factors that influence your score to ensuring timely payments of loans, every aspect of credit management has been precisely covered.

As you navigate the details of loan approval, remember that you don't have to go it alone. At **People Financials,** we're here to support you every step of the way. Whether you're exploring loan-seeking personalized guidance offline, our team of financial experts is dedicated to helping you make informed decisions.

From assessing your financial needs to choosing the right loan product, our experts at **People Financials** will work tirelessly to tailor a loan solution that meets your unique requirements. With our extensive network of trusted lenders and unparalleled expertise, we're committed to guiding you toward financial success.

So, if you're ready to take control of your financial future and unlock the doors to greater opportunities, reach out to us at **People Financials** Together, let's embark on a journey toward financial mastery and pave the way for a brighter tomorrow.

Remember, your path to loan approval starts here, with **"Loan Approval Simplified"** as your trusted companion and **People Financials** as your partner in financial empowerment.

Email id: hello@prabhatagrawal.com

Website: prabhatagrawal.com

Phone no: 9599416000

Address:

213, Ansal Tower-38, Nehru Place, New Delhi -110019